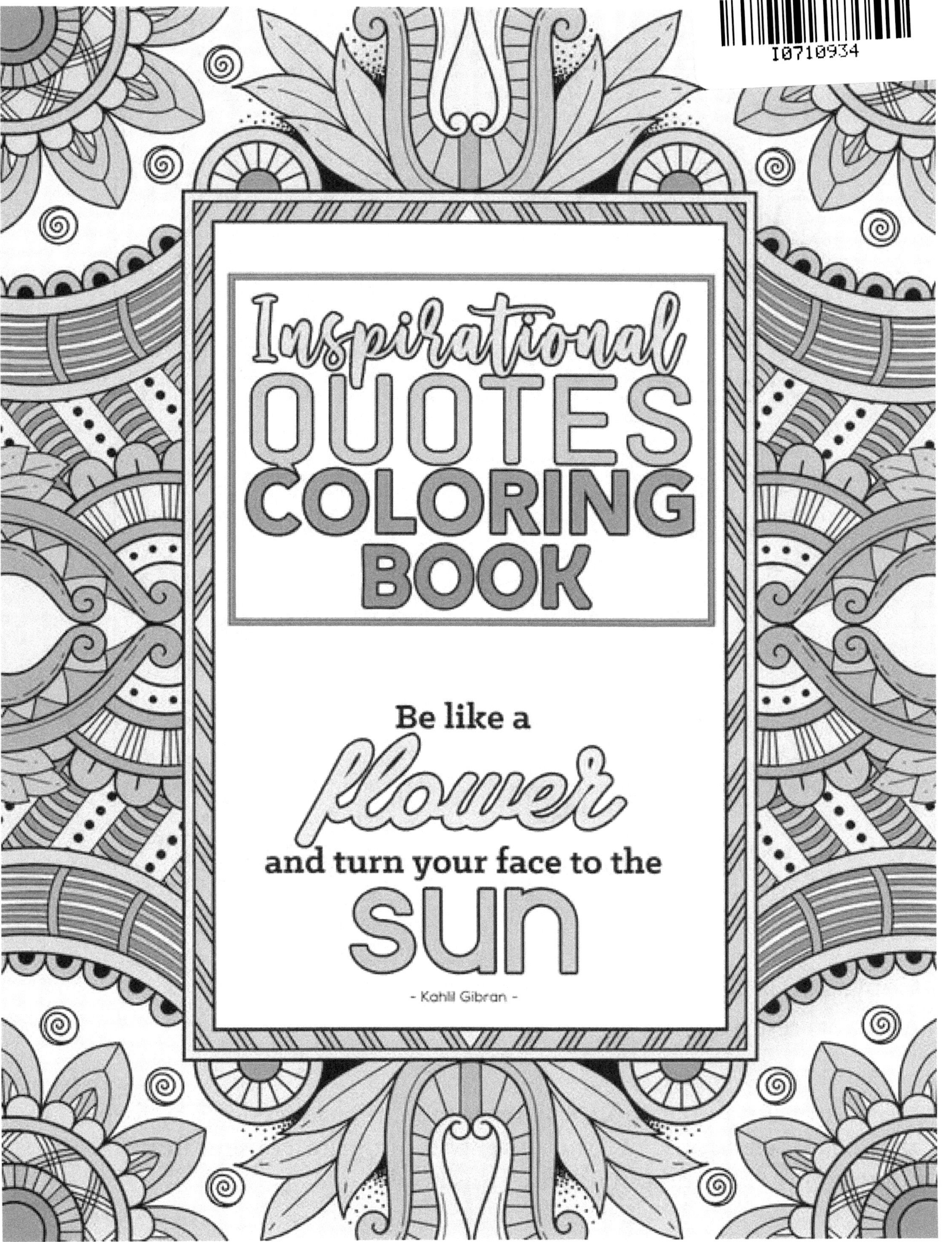
Inspirational
QUOTES
COLORING
BOOK

Be like a
flower
and turn your face to the
sun
- Kahlil Gibran -

If you have only one smile in you
GIVE IT
to the people you
LOVE
- Maya Angelou -

Love is our true destiny.
We do not find the meaning of LIFE by ourselves alone - we find it with another.
- Thomas Merton

A heart is not judged by how much you
LOVE,
but by how much you are
LOVED BY OTHERS
- Frank Morgan -

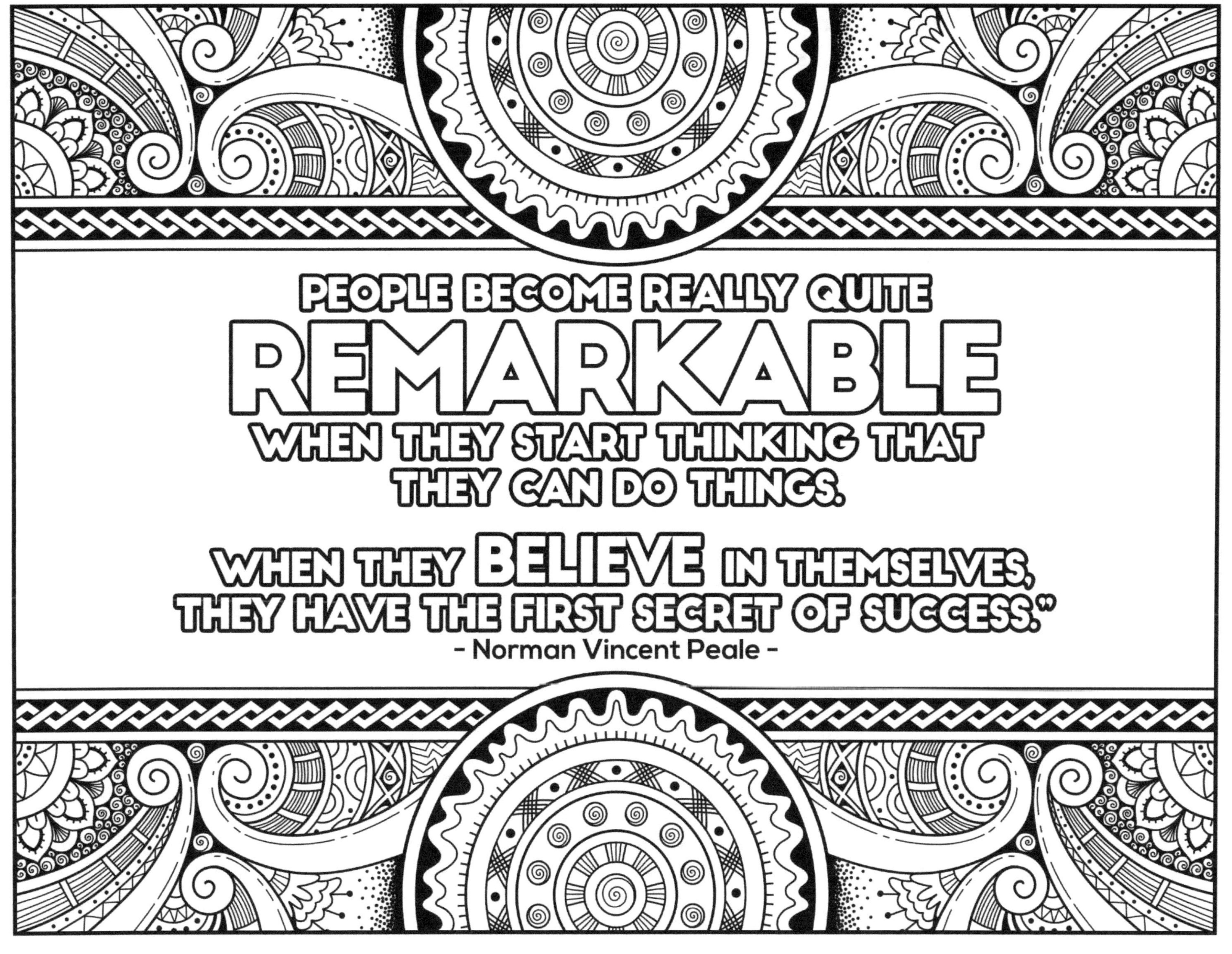

PEOPLE BECOME REALLY QUITE
REMARKABLE
WHEN THEY START THINKING THAT
THEY CAN DO THINGS.
WHEN THEY BELIEVE IN THEMSELVES,
THEY HAVE THE FIRST SECRET OF SUCCESS."
- Norman Vincent Peale -

Live daringly, boldly, fearlessly.
Taste the relish to be found in
COMPETITION
in having put forth the best within you.
- Henry J. Kaiser -

Be like a
flower
and turn your face to the
sun
- Kahlil Gibran -

BE THANKFUL
for what you have; you'll end up
HAVING MORE
If you concentrate on what you don't have,
YOU WILL NEVER, EVER HAVE ENOUGH.
- Oprah Winfrey

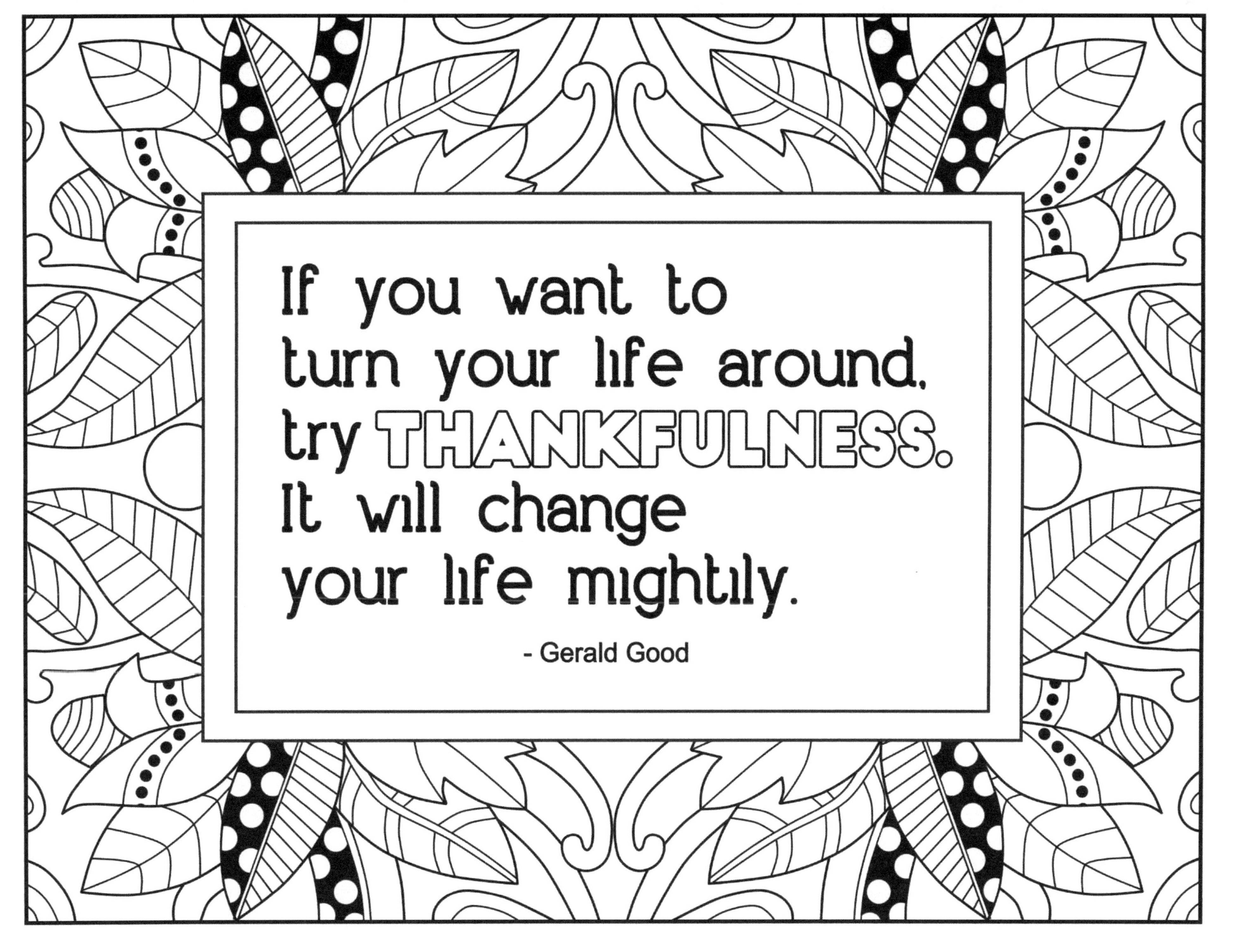
If you want to
turn your life around,
try THANKFULNESS.
It will change
your life mightily.
- Gerald Good

Luck,
that's when preparation
and opportunity
MEET.
- Pierre Trudeau

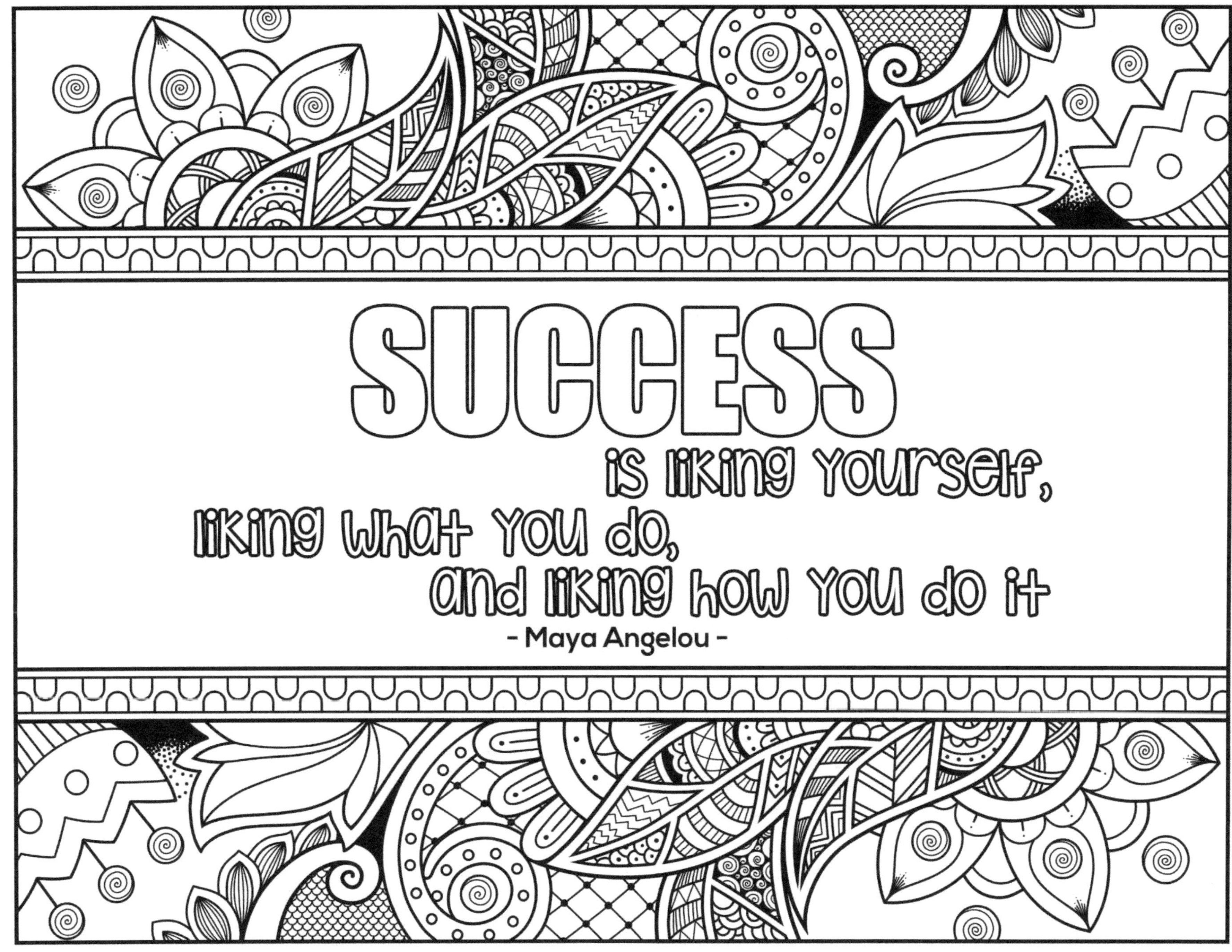

SUCCESS
is liking yourself,
liking what you do,
and liking how you do it
- Maya Angelou -

Success is not the key to happiness. Happiness is the key to success. If you love what you are doing, you will be successful.
- Albert Schweitzer -

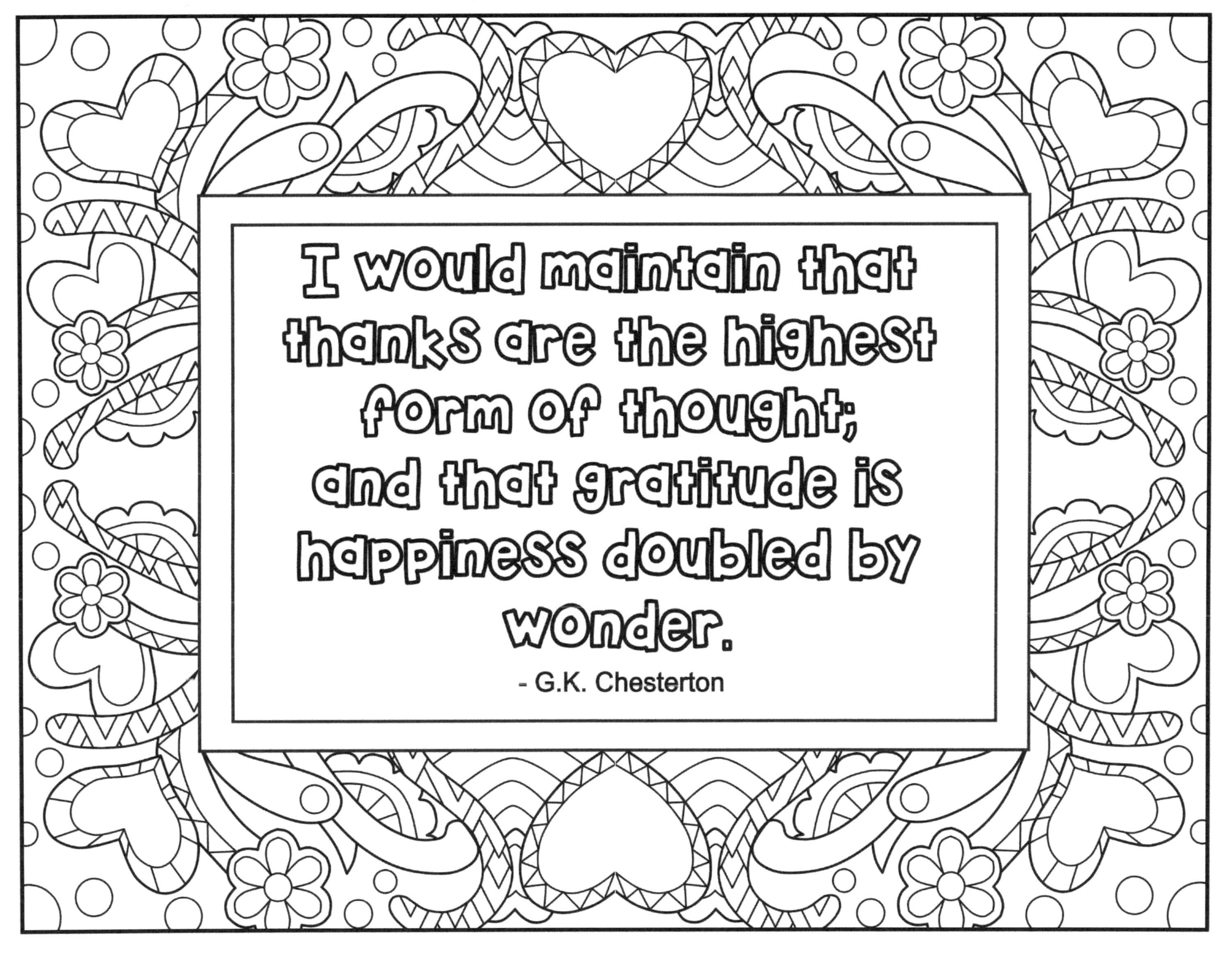

I would maintain that thanks are the highest form of thought; and that gratitude is happiness doubled by wonder.
- G.K. Chesterton

Each day is a gift from God.
What you do with it is
your gift to Him.
- T.D. Jakes

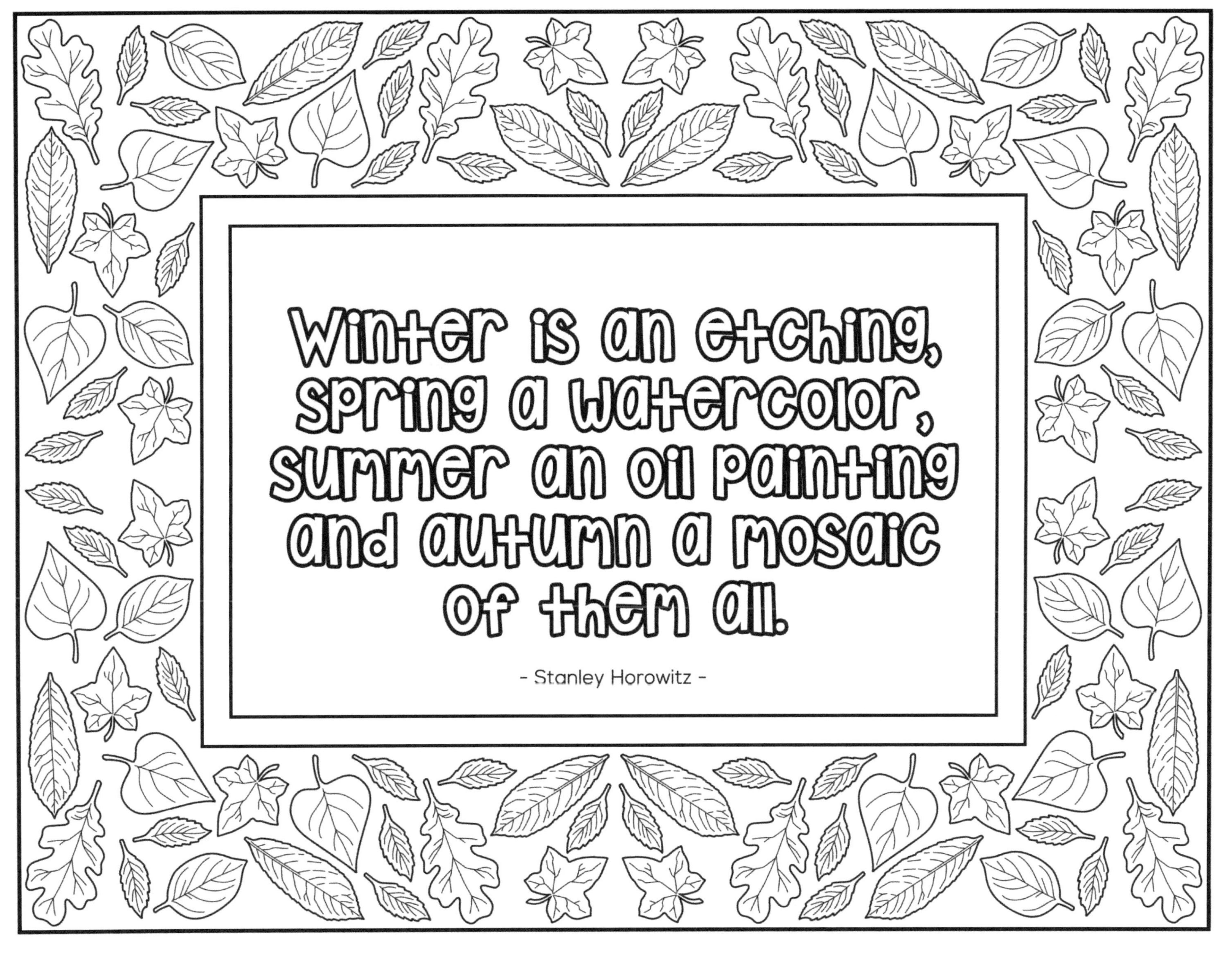

Winter is an etching,
spring a watercolor,
summer an oil painting
and autumn a mosaic
of them all.
- Stanley Horowitz -

It
does not matter
how slowly you go,
so long as you
DO NOT STOP
- Confucius -

DO WHAT IS RIGHT
NOT WHAT IS EASY

I WOULD RATHER SIT ON A PUMPKIN AND HAVE IT ALL TO MYSELF, THAN BE CROWDED ON A VELVET CUSHION
- Henry David Thoreau -

Tis the last rose of summer,
Left blooming alone;
All her lovely companions
Are faded and gone.

- Thomas Moore, The Last Rose of Summer,

THE SUN JUST TOUCHED THE MORNING;
THE MORNING, HAPPY THING,
SUPPOSED THAT HE HAD COME TO DWELL,
AND LIFE WOULD BE ALL SPRING.
– Emily Dickinson –

The Summer looks out
from her brazen tower,
Through the
flashing bars of July.
– Francis Thompson, A Corymbus for Autumn